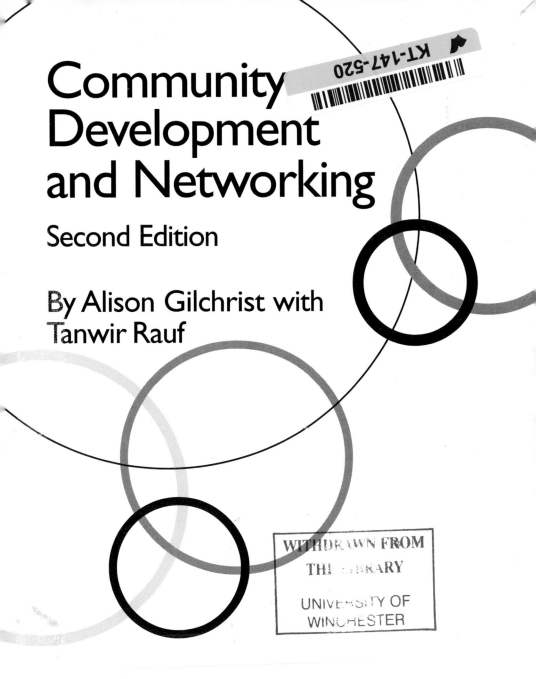

Community Development and Networking

Second Edition

By Alison Gilchrist with
Tanwir Rauf

community
development
foundation

First Published in Great Britain in 2006 by the
Community Development Foundation
Unit 5, Angel Gate
320–326 City Road
London EC1V 2PT
Registered charity number 306130
in association with
Community Development Exchange
Floor 4, Furnival House
48 Furnival Gate
Sheffield S1 4QP

British Library Cataloguing-in-Publication Data
A record of this publication is available from the British Library.

ISBN 1 901974 67 7

Typesetting by Bearcomm.com, Penzance 01736 333355
Printed in Great Britain by Elmtree Graphics, Colchester

Contents

Community Development Foundation (CDF)

The Community Development Foundation, set up in 1968, helps communities achieve greater control over the conditions and decisions affecting their lives by:

- advising government and other bodies on measures to build strong, active communities and promote community development and involvement

- supporting community work of all kinds through networks, links with practitioners, and collaborative work with partner organisations and management of local projects

- carrying out research, evaluation and policy analysis to identify good practice in all aspects of community development and involvement, and disseminating lessons through training, conferences, publications and consultancy.

CDF is a leading authority on community development in the UK and Europe. It is a non-departmental public body supported mainly by the Active Communities Directorate of the Home Office with substantial backing from local government, charitable trusts and the private sector. The Community Development Foundation is committed to openness in its affairs, apart from where bound by the need for confidentiality.

Community Development Foundation
Unit 5, Angel Gate
320–326 City Road
London EC1V 2PT
Tel: 020 7226 5375
Fax: 020 7704 0313
Email: admin@cdf.org.uk
Website: www.cdf.org.uk

Registered Charity Number 306130

Community Development Exchange

Formerly known as the Standing Conference for Community Development (SCCD), CDX is the UK-wide membership organisation for community development.

CDX works to ensure that community development (CD) is recognised and supported as a powerful way of tackling inequality and achieving social justice. As an organisation with members from across England, Scotland, Wales and Northern Ireland, CDX reflects a diverse range of interests in community development across all sectors and fields.

Community Development Exchange
Floor 4, Furnival House
48 Furnival Gate
Sheffield S1 4QP
Tel: 0114 270 1718
Email: admin@cdx.org.uk
Website: www.cdx.org.uk

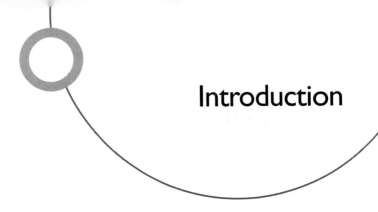

Introduction

In recent years there has been a growing interest among community workers and other professionals in the practice of **networking** and the development and use of **networks**. Like 'community', the concept of 'networking' is in danger of losing its meaning and becoming a catch-all phrase for any kind of conversation or loose association of people. The value of networking as an efficient and legitimate method of community work needs to be properly understood and recognised by people involved in training, funding, managing and practising community development.

This booklet aims to provide the beginnings of a theoretical framework for practitioners, policymakers and managers in the field of community development. It argues that networking should be seen as a core process of community development. This will encourage a more conscious use of the **craft** of networking and affirm the value of networks in supporting collective organisation and communication.

The first section gives a broad overview of how networks and networking contribute to the community development process. Section 2 explores the ways in which informal and formal networks can support community development and raises some questions about the nature of different kinds of umbrella organisations. Section 3 focuses on networking as a method of community development. It sets out the main techniques for achieving equality of opportunity. Section 4 uses some practical examples to illustrate flexible methods of organisation to overcome barriers to communication and co-operation. The concluding section reviews some of the main issues around networking as a method of community development and makes recommendations as to how networking can be encouraged through practical support and professional recognition.

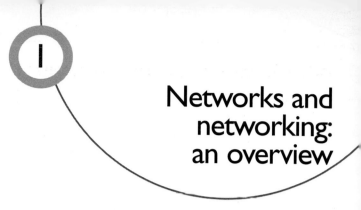

Networks and networking: an overview

What is networking?

Networking is the process by which relationships and contacts between people or organisations are established, nurtured and utilised for mutual benefit. These personal connections often give rise to community campaigns and self-help initiatives, which may also evolve into more structured organisations, providing the range of services and consultation mechanisms which characterise the voluntary and community sector. Informal links between individuals and organisations provide an important means by which people gain access to ideas, information, opinions, resources and expertise which would not otherwise be directly available. Networking allows this potential to be released for individual advantage or for the benefit of the wider community, and thus can be empowering for those involved. It can also, however, be exclusive, as in the classic 'old boys' networks', used to maintain privilege and stereotypical attitudes. Networking for community development is concerned about opening up opportunities for all, and must include strategies for positive action to challenge discrimination and inequality.

It is useful to make a distinction between the **process** of networking, as described at the beginning of this section, and networks as **organisational forms**. The *process* of networking is about developing and using human relationships. A *network*, as such, consists of the set of relationships between people who have direct and indirect connections with each other. Networks might be very loosely organised around friendship or kin groups, with only informal rules of interaction. Alternatively, networks can be quite formally structured, with a written constitution and democratically agreed aims. Networks offer a means of initiating and sustaining contacts between individuals and groups, without necessarily requiring the formality of meetings, official membership or a constitution.

What is community development?

As Marilyn Taylor states in the first Briefing Paper of this series, 'Community development is about change and growth'. It 'works both within communities and across the boundaries between communities and the institutions that affect them' (Taylor and West, 2001, p.6). The Community Development Exchange defines community development as 'about building active and sustainable communities based on social justice and mutual respect' (SCCD, 2001, p.5). It goes on to say that 'It is about changing power structures to remove the barriers that prevent people from participating in the issues that affect their lives'. Community development is about working with people in ways that help them to have greater influence over important decisions, and to come together with others to devise solutions to common problems. By enabling people to share their skills and knowledge, community development promotes learning through informal and social education. Community development aims to help people make connections between their own lives and wider policy issues through a cycle of action, reflection and learning. It is based on a recognition that collective action is more influential than a series of single voices, and that co-operation between people generates a shared strength through the pooling of energy ideas and resources.

Networking for the 21st century

Networking as a recognised way of working emerged in Britain towards the end of the 1980s. Incorporating concepts from information technology, it reflected political trends and the gathering momentum of certain social movements that had emerged during the previous two decades. Many groups felt marginalised by traditional forms of association and political representation. They began to organise separately, on the basis of their identity and experience of oppression as women, black people, gay men, lesbians and bisexuals, older people and, most recently, disabled people. This was a positive experience for many people and community work was strongly influenced by these critical perspectives. 'Positive action' projects were set up to support the self-organisation and empowerment of different groups who felt themselves to be oppressed in this society, and these were important elements in the political struggles for recognition and equality during this period. Too often, however, groups appeared to compete for funding and attention, which led to a frustrating sense of isolation and division within the community development movement.

A way needed to be found of overcoming this fragmentation, and networking has recently gained currency as a form of association and communication. By enabling people to maintain their own identities and yet work together across organisational and identity boundaries, it encourages diversity and allows the development of strong alliances around particular issues.

Networking has the potential to transform current inequalities because it creates the possibility for information, expertise and influence to flow across organisational and cultural barriers. This affords access for disadvantaged individuals and smaller community groups to resources and support that might not otherwise be available to them. Feelings of oppression and hostility can be counteracted through direct experience and positive role models. Direct and indirect discrimination can be combated by joint campaigning, education, debate and negotiation.

This is particularly important for developing greater cohesion in society and in helping different organisations to work together in partnership (Gilchrist, 2004a). Research shows that good interpersonal relationships based on trust and mutual understanding provide a vital foundation when disagreements or tensions arise between people with diverse agendas and perspectives (Gilchrist, 2004b). This collective resource is sometimes called **social capital**, and comprises the networks and norms that people develop through their associations and informal interaction with others.

The case for networking

Networking offers a simple means of communicating across quite complicated patterns of relationships and organisation. Networks have five main functions:

- information exchange
- developing relationships of support and solidarity
- developing a sense of community purpose on the basis of shared values and identity
- providing a forum for debate and discussion
- negotiating and articulating a collective view on issues which are relevant to participating members.

Networks are a potent form of organisation whenever co-operation between a diverse set of individuals or groups is desirable. In particular, networks provide opportunities for partnership with more powerful bodies, which smaller community organisations might not be able to achieve and sustain on their own. They also facilitate the organisation of joint projects or events, which promote the shared interests of a number of agencies and allow common perspectives to be put forward, for example, through community engagement strategies.

Many community-based charities directly benefit from membership of an independent network, through which they or their allies can lobby and campaign on overtly political issues without compromising their charitable status.

Networking as a core process of community development

The main purpose of community development is to enable people to work together in egalitarian and democratic ways to develop collective solutions to shared problems.

Networking is fundamental to this process, and community workers are often instrumental in helping an informal network to evolve into something more open, that can ensure access for all those who might benefit from membership or collaboration. This is particularly the case for organisations and community representatives involved in formal partnerships, for example managing regeneration programmes or crime reduction strategies.

Maintaining good working contacts and nurturing positive relations between people provide the foundation for community development at a number of levels. Network members learn from one another, increasing their own skills, knowledge and confidence. Sharing experience and ideas in a supportive environment between people from different backgrounds and professional perspectives promotes mutual respect and understanding. Community workers can contribute to this and learn from it.

The use of networks and networking is both an expression of the values of community development and a means by which community development is achieved.

Networking provides opportunities for collective activity and solidarity to emerge within an alliance of different individuals and organisations without requiring that people 'lose' their chosen identities, allegiances and different interests. It is a valuable means of developing strength through diversity. Crucially, it enables a badly needed identity to emerge for the 'community sector' itself, which can campaign and advocate for policy developments from a local community action perspective. Within different sections of the population (whether these are based on locality, identity or interest) a sense of common purpose and mutual interaction develops, providing a solid foundation for the development of 'community capacity'. This 'capacity building' is further enhanced by the way networks overlap with, or even provide the mechanisms for, consultation and collective decision-making.

In recent years, government policies have emphasised the value of community engagement in planning, developing and delivering a whole raft of initiatives aimed at improving the quality of life, especially within disadvantaged communities (Chanan, 2003). For communities to be involved in wider decision-making arrangements (for example around health or planning issues), there needs to be some investment in the formal and informal infrastructure that enables communities to identify, debate and articulate their own needs and aspirations so that they can better participate in partnership and service delivery. Networks within communities are essential to supporting and holding community representatives to account, as well as encouraging new people to come forward for these roles. The government's civil renewal and active citizenship programmes are about using community development values and methods, along with the work of 'anchor' organisations to build community capacity in every area (CRU, 2004). However, many areas do not have such a body, and in many instances community development involves much more dispersed work, supporting participation and helping to make connections among people who find it difficult to meet up for very practical reasons. Local and issue-based forums are effective means of bringing together people who have a common interest, but it should be recognised that informal networks are also useful in gathering views from people who are not so well-organised or who are unable to attend formal meetings, such as homeless people, refugees and asylum seekers or young people.

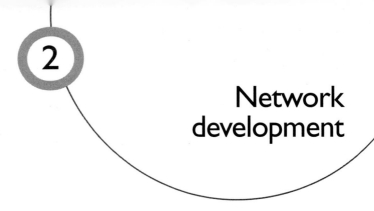

Network development

This section addresses the issue of how community workers can use and develop networks to promote and work towards the aims of community development. How can networks be assisted to make the transition from information connections between individuals to the setting up of democratic structures which meet community needs? Two different, but related themes are considered:

● networking as a process of making and using contacts

● developing networks as structures and communication systems.

The process of networking – serendipity and strategic opportunism

Sometimes networking is intentional and deliberate, as when people contact one another for specific purposes. Other times it occurs through unplanned conversations or chance encounters. This happens time and time again and will be recognised by many community workers as a valid and effective aspect of their practice. A word that ideally captures the unpremeditated nature of these processes is **serendipity**, or making the most of unforeseen opportunities. It is a key aspect of networking which acknowledges the beneficial outcomes of accidental meetings and the capacity to make connections and discoveries through such 'happenstance' coincidences. These serendipitous aspects of networking involve 'luck breaks', which cannot be predicted, but often prove extremely advantageous. Examples are a chance introduction at a purely social event or bumping into some in the course of everyday life, such as when shopping or at the swimming pool.

Community workers often adopt a slightly more purposeful tactic, which increases the time spent at events and places where they are likely to meet useful and interesting people. This approach might be termed **strategic opportunism** or 'being in the right place at the right time'. It underpins a more intentional approach to building contacts, even though it might be difficult to predict exactly which connections will be made or prove beneficial.

Informal networks in the community

Informal networks consist of the variety of personal and professional relationships that connect individuals and organisations in casual, but usually positive ways. These informal networks operate in 'ordinary' life and constitute an important aspect of people's sense of belonging to a 'community'. Informal networks rarely have a clearly defined membership or boundaries. They constantly change and expand by making connections with other networks, and as strangers become acquaintances and then possibly friends, colleagues or even kin!

Informal networks are not constituted in any legal or structural sense but provide important communications systems in society. In particular, such informal networks offer vital means of access to influence, resources, opportunities and information. They tend to be based on shared interests, beliefs, values and identity, but are affected by locality in that people who are familiar with each other are often more likely to strike up conversation and form a connection.

Such links gradually develop into more sustained relationships, in which people offer each other support, exchange items of gossip and news, and talk about the problems they are experiencing. These and other forms of practical assistance are the seedbed of many a campaign or self-help project. Apparently private problems are redefined as public issues, requiring a collective solution. Many local community initiatives will have been conceived outside the school gates and nurtured over the kitchen table!

Informal networks also provide fruitful channels of communication by which information percolates through the community. However, they cannot be guaranteed to operate in non-discriminatory ways. By their very nature, 'grapevines' are personal to those involved and will only reach certain sections of the community. It is vital that community development workers are able to identify the many networks that exist within communities and are also aware of where these are likely to intersect or conflict.

Maintaining informal workers

Networks consist of a web of links between individuals and organisations. It is important to nurture these relationships so that the network of useful contacts remains positive, relevant and up-to-date. The maintenance of networks is about 'staying in touch' in ways that are not particularly purposeful but which ensure that people will respond favourably to a request for help at some future date. The sending of greetings cards (for Eid, Christmas, birthdays or whatever) is one method of reminding one another of community goodwill. Attendance at annual general meetings demonstrates support and interest in the work of our respective projects. Stopping to chat after meetings or on the street enables friends and colleagues to stay abreast of each other's news and views, whilst the occasional phone call, e-mail or letter lets someone know that you want to stay in contact and value their support or professional opinion.

Networks as communication systems

Networks provide excellent channels for communication. In community work, personal connections are crucial, dependent on knowing who's who, their likely views on key issues and where they can be reached.

For example, different networks in a local neighbourhood can be used to carry information about plans for a community festival. As well as using traditional publicity media such as posters, press releases and local newsletters, the community worker will make a point of talking to a number of key individuals, such as local artists and performers, playworkers and others who might be expected to make a contribution. The worker will encourage these people to talk with others they know who might be interested, and gradually the word will spread through the community.

In order to do this successfully, the worker needs to be aware of how these communication channels operate in the neighbourhood and take steps to ensure that all sections of the community are reached. This may involve a strategy of deliberately contacting people from each of the minority ethnic populations in the area or making sure that disabled people (who might be isolated from the 'mainstream' community) will hear about and feel welcome to contribute to the initiative. The community worker needs to know the interconnecting points between networks, and avoid the 'dead-ends' if at all possible. The choice of the messenger can be significant. Someone who is respected by other members of their network will be in a better position to convey information and to influence opinion.

Use of a regular mailing or newsletter provides a simple and efficient method by which members of networks can exchange information of general relevance.

Similarly, up-to-date and comprehensive contact lists (with names, addresses, e-mails and telephone numbers) ensure that individuals and organisations in the networks can be in touch over matters of specific interest. Producing a directory of local organisations can be an excellent way of developing networks. The internet and computer technology such as databases, web-based discussion groups, e-mailings and telephone conferencing facilities can assist in gathering information and tracing connections, especially where potential network members are not already known to each other.

Creating new networks

Community workers are often involved in innovative work where the groundwork of contact building has not been carried out. At an early stage it is useful to signal an interest or intention to the world at large in order to make contact with potential co-operators and allies. Press releases or letters to the local press and broadcasting media can alter the public's reaction to your proposal. Additionally, articles or flyers sent out through more specialised mailings and newsletters, targeted at particular identity or interest groups, will find their way into already established networks. People might be invited to a meeting or simply to register their interest with a contact person. A list of interested parties can then be drawn up and extended to form the basis of a new network, deliberately created with a specific purpose of mind.

This 'broadcast' approach to networking can be supplemented by a more focused 'stepping-stone' or 'snowballing' technique of using existing contacts to identify potential members of a new network and then sounding these out through systematic, but unpredictable conversations based on the initial suggestion and subsequent introductions.

Network transformation – the role for community development

The value of networks and networking can only be realised for community development purposes if community workers understand the practical implications of this approach and are equipped with the necessary skills in communication, organisation and anti-discriminatory practices to ensure that networking is effective and non-oppressive.

Community development workers have a key role to play in helping networks form. They put people in touch with each other, set up introductions and generally encourage them to develop their own set of contacts within the community. This role has been termed 'meta-networking' and refers specifically to situations where the worker intervenes as either a 'connector' or a 'catalyst' to help people to work better across boundaries and barriers (see Gilchrist, 1998, 2004a). This may involve simply signposting individuals to other organisations, or dealing with difficulties and differences between groups that are not used to working together (for example providing interpreting or conflict mediation). Meta-networking is about helping others to maintain and manage their own web of relationships so that the community worker can withdraw from active involvement and move onto other things.

One strategy employed by community workers is to increase the number of opportunities for direct meetings and conversation between people in the community, such as regular, but informal meetings or social events. A research study by Chanan (1992) of community activity across several countries in Europe has demonstrated that this stage of informal networking is highly productive in laying the bedrock of future voluntary initiatives and self-help activities. Similarly, research by CDF of one of its projects (Bell, 1992) demonstrated how many community projects emerge both from the casual interactions of local relationships and conversations, as well as more directly from formalised networks. This serendipitous aspect of networking and the lack of formal organisation are an important part of the background 'chatter' of community interaction. Community development workers use this as a foundation for bringing people together around shared needs and aspirations. By providing a forum for discussion, networks encourage a sense of community, which can supply the strength and common identity for lobbying and joint initiatives. The features that make networks strong and vibrant – their diversity, openness and flexibility – make them valuable vehicles for community development.

Emerging structures

Community development can intervene in this environment by actively helping networks to evolve. Although people probably do read posters and community newsletters, it is likely that initial contacts with community groups and activities arise through conversation with other individuals who are already involved in some way. Informal communication and connections within the community provides a shared capacity for information exchange and problem solving, and it can make sense to formalise this. The individuals involved value the relationships they have with each other and seek ways to consolidate them. This might include the setting up of regular, but still informal, opportunities for meeting and sharing contact names and addresses, perhaps through a directory or mailing list, or through a regular lunch-club type event.

Networking for equality and empowerment

It is also important to recognise that networking offers a method of empowering sections of the community who experience inequality and deprivation. Solidarity networks often evolve of their own accord but can become more effective if coaxed into more formal structures, such as self-organised associations and support or advocacy groups. These can then provide strength and a common voice with which to demand resources, rights of access and participation in the wider community. The basis for these 'counter-networks' will often be a common experience of discrimination. By being in touch with one another, members of these groups can develop positive identities, a collective strength and powerful influence which would not have been possible if dispersed throughout the whole community. They provide a challenge to the norms and stereotypes operating in society. Moreover, these networks are likely to include members who are connected into other organisations and can act as 'bridges', enabling everyone else to gain access to useful information and resources.

Recognising the limitations of networks

The concept of the 'tyranny of structurelessness' (derived from critiques of the early British women's liberation movement) is applicable to networks. This is especially true of those organisations that have no formal mechanisms or policies for resolving disagreements or challenging inequalities. It is common for those who feel more confident and articulate to dominate discussion and decision-making (often without realising it) and for well-intentioned but elitist cliques to emerge. This tendency is typical of many forms of collective organisation that do not actively address power differentials and inequalities within their own membership.

It is sometimes compounded by the lack of internal accountability and agreed procedures for making decisions. Some members will choose to involve themselves actively in meetings and working parties; others will simply attend and listen. Many will only have time to receive and contribute to a newsletter or network mailing. The level of activity by each individual or organisation will depend on the perceived usefulness of the network, and the amount of spare capacity which people have left over from their other commitments. As a result, the responsibility for servicing the network sometimes falls on a core group of just a few individuals who may come to be seen as a controlling clique. This tension is experienced by many networks and needs to be addressed through collective discussion and a willingness constantly to review the allocation of organisational tasks and representation. It is a major limitation for networks, which is explored in more depth in Section 3.

Democratic tensions

Formally constituted networks generally fulfil their main functions through regular open meetings, where information is exchanged, issues debated and decisions taken by all those present. Usually these decisions will be reached through discussion and consensus, but occasionally a vote may have to be taken. This raises questions of democratic control and accountability. Whilst the agreed view may commit the network to a particular position or action, it is unlikely to have a binding influence or mandate on members to carry out the policy. Whether or not the decision is implemented will depend, crucially, on whether the individuals and organisations respect the outcome and take action as a result. The lack of formal democratic mechanisms for deciding a policy on every issue often results in a rather precarious approach to 'representation' and consultation with outside bodies. There is a danger that the opinions articulated reflect the ideas of only the most vociferous and active individuals in the network, rather than the views and interests of the majority. The recent experience of community empowerment networks and various forms of local strategic partnerships suggest that this is a common problem that will require more time and more community development work before they can become properly representative.

Finding the right size and structure

Human factors, such as trust, loyalty and respect, influence the nature and quality of direct communication and interpersonal relationships. These are vital aspects of networking, especially in the community development field. Consequently, there are limits to the size of organisation that can function as a loose collective on the basis of minimal co-ordination. When this stage is reached (which probably reflects the natural growth of a successful network), it may be appropriate for the organisation to make a clear decision to change itself, either by adopting a more formalised structure or by separating itself into several component parts, each with a different focus. These can then maintain contact with one another, perhaps through a forum-type organisation.

It may be the case that networks can only function effectively up to a certain 'critical mass'. Beyond that level difficulties begin to appear, perhaps because the relationships between members become too remote and impersonal. Another explanation may relate to the lack of democratic procedures of many networks. Where networks do not have mechanisms for managing differences of opinion, disagreements fester within the membership, emerging at a later stage as organisational or personality conflicts which contaminate the entire fragile web of relationships. Networks may need to change into new structures once they reach a certain size, when conflicts and clashes are more likely to arise but the means for resolving disagreements are not available. A pattern of network breakdown is beginning to emerge, which suggests that once an optimum size of about 40 active participants is passed, a network tends to disintegrate into smaller sub-groups. Alternatively, in order to carry on effectively with a membership of more than this number, the network may have to transform itself into a more centralised organisation, containing the beginnings of a structural hierarchy, such as a steering group or, eventually, an executive committee.

Networks as umbrella organisations

Among the many forms of organisation that bring people together for a common purpose, networks offer a particular means of association. They allow participants to retain much of their own identity and autonomy, whilst supporting joint initiatives and the sharing of experience. Different levels of engagement and formality are required, depending on whether the association is based on simple information exchange, or whether greater degrees of co-ordination, co-operation and collaboration are desired. Intermediary bodies, such as rural community councils or councils for voluntary service, can play a vital role in setting up and supporting networks around specific issues (such as transport) or identities (carers). The recent government cross-cutting review looking at the role of the voluntary and community sectors in service delivery in England and Wales has resulted in increased funding for infrastructure organisations through the Change Up programme. Similar approaches have been adopted in Scotland and Northern Ireland. This is a useful form of investment but probably doesn't go far enough in helping such bodies with their networking functions.

Other organisational models – a comparison

There are many examples in community development of organisations working together to set up joint projects over the short term or to liaise on a more regular basis for support, and to provide a platform from which a collective view can be articulated.

Umbrella organisations take different forms, depending on their main purpose. Usually they will have clearly defined aims and a constitution that specifies who may become members and how decisions will be made. Most associations tend to acquire their own identifiable 'core' function, which can often develop an identity of its own, separate from the actual membership. Each of the different types of organisation identified below may have evolved from an initial networking stage, but they have developed a structure which is appropriate to the functions they currently perform, even though most will still support some elements of networking. By contrast, a network is characterised as a particular type of multi-member association, which is fairly flexibly organised, operates with a minimal central core, has a relatively flat, loose democratic structure, and encourages direct and indirect connections between the participating organisations and individuals.

Federations tend to consist of similar types of organisations, such as tenants' associations or sports clubs. They allow the member groups to operate independently, and to share information and ideas about their broadly identical functions. They may also have a representative function in relation to specific consultation processes, for example in relation to planning applications.

Forums and voluntary established councils might be made up of diverse groups with a strong common focus. The organisation will have a democratic life of its own, with policies, structures and medium-term goals which have a distinct accountability towards the member organisations. Examples might be around qualifications for childcare and early years learning, or the regional voluntary sector networks that provide a platform across England for voluntary organisations to influence the policies and programmes of government offices and the regional development agencies.

Coalitions and alliances are different again in that they are more goal-oriented, often set up around a particular issue or project. These usually develop from initial informal networking that has enabled people to identify sympathetic contacts and potential allies. An example might be of several groups and individuals getting together to set up a local nursery facility or to promote the cause of disability equality. The coalition may stop functioning once the initial goal has been achieved or it may transform itself into a now more appropriate structure, such as a project management committee or advisory panel.

Consortiums are multi-agency bodies set up to achieve a definite purpose, such as the management of a bulk-buy co-operative. In this respect, co-operation is primarily task-oriented and focused on achieving a very specific goal.

Formal networks may have agreed aims and objectives, and definite criteria for membership, which still allow differences between the members to flourish. Networks differ from other multi-agency bodies in that they are rarely goal-oriented and often have a highly varied membership, united solely by a very broad common purpose. For example, a city-wide network of community groups might include small neighbourhood-based groups, local intermediary agencies, city farms, campaigning bodies, service-oriented organisations, county-wide coalitions, and training agencies. Meetings might be attended by activists, professional community workers, volunteers and other paid officers from a range of voluntary and statutory agencies. The arena created by such meetings provides opportunities for people to exchange information and discuss issues, bringing a range of perspectives and expertise to the debate. Participants share common ground in their commitment to maintaining the voluntary and community sectors, participating in the network as nominal equals, although they may disagree over a number of other issues.

Finally, **partnerships** have become a familiar, if sometimes frustrating, aspect of community life, overseeing the planning and delivery of government programmes across a wide range of policies. Partnerships are formally constituted arrangements that enable different sectors and agencies to co-ordinate their activities, pool resources and negotiate ways of meeting community needs as well as achieving government targets. They enable various services to work better together by requiring joint decision-making and identifying opportunities for collaboration.

It is useful to compare these types of organisations and consider how they differ in relation to three important dimensions:

- the degree to which they have been set up to achieve a particular goal
- the relative diversity of membership
- the level of democratic accountability between the membership and the organisation.

The degree of formality or flexibility with which the organisation functions is also an important factor. When considering the nature of organisation that might be suited to different purposes it may be useful to think in terms of the following table.

	Goals	Diversity	Accountability
Federations	Medium	Low	Medium
Forums	Medium/High	Low	Low
Councils	Medium	Medium	High
Coalitions and alliances	High	High	Medium
Consortiums	High	Medium	Low
Networks	Low	High	Low
Partnerships	High	High	High

This categorisation is not intended to prescribe rigid definitions for different kinds of associations. Rather it offers a guide as to which forms of organisation are most appropriate for different purposes. It also suggests that some structures are not suitable for certain functions. Consultation exercises that are seeking consensus or a representative view are not best served by the sometimes muddled accountabilities of networks. On the other hand, the diverse membership of networks ensures stimulating discussion across a broad spectrum of groups and individuals. As such, they are a rich source of ideas and are excellent for generating a sense of the range of different perspectives around a particular issue. Positive action measures (see next section) are particularly important in ensuring that minority interests have some influence, enabling hidden voices to emerge.

Community development encourages forms of self-organisation that provide support, services and opportunities for democratic participation in the community. In the Community Development Exchange (CDX) *Strategic Framework for Community Development,* networking is described as a means of providing strategic support to communities and enabling co-operation between different agencies 'through the development of trust and understanding' (SCCD, 2001, p. 20). This is dependent on investing in both organisational links and personal relationships, and not leaving this to chance or those rare moments when nothing else takes priority.

This section has illustrated how networks enable people to come together, identify a common cause, and mobilise resources within and beyond the community which can be used for collective problem-solving and to further social justice.

3

Good practice and the craft of networking

This section looks at how the skills, knowledge and understanding of networking can be applied to promote community development aims. A key feature of community development is that co-operation and collective approaches are encouraged and often workers find themselves in pivotal roles, co-ordinating and servicing initiatives involving several agencies from different sectors. An ability to network effectively is essential to this process and this approach should of course be informed by community development principles around equality and empowerment. The current emphasis within government policies on community participation and partnership working means that skills and strategies that help people work together across organisational and sectoral boundaries are particularly valuable. This refers to multi-agency working, for example between health professionals, the police, housing officers and so on, where different organisational aims and cultures can make it difficult to find a common language, let alone a common purpose. For people involved in community development work, it is vital that community leaders and representatives have networks that will provide support and hold them accountable.

Mapping and building contacts through the community

One of the dangers of using informal networks to convey information through a community is that people are as liable to suppress or discredit a message as to convey it reliably and intact. To reduce the likelihood of messages going astray or turning themselves into gossipy rumours, community workers must understand how informal networks transmit information and be able to recognise when more formal channels of communication are appropriate. Networks tend to be held together not by organisational conventions, but by rather more personal factors, such as shared values and interests. They can become over-dependent on the biases and whims of individuals, thereby losing democratic credibility. This can result in exclusive cliques developing that block information flow and seek to maintain their own power and privilege.

Getting to know people

Community work involves a great deal of conversation. Chatting to people who drop in to the office, on the street, over a cup of tea after a meeting or on a home visit is a vital and enjoyable aspect of the job. But this is not simply aimless 'passing the time of day'. There is an underlying, often unacknowledged purpose to such conversations, which is to find out more about that person – what interests them, what skills they have, what resources they have at their disposal, who they know, what activities they might be involved in, how they see the issues affecting their community, what are their aspirations and what ideas they have for achieving these.

This 'constructive chatting' is part of the community worker's craft and has at least two functions. The first is about establishing and nurturing positive relationships; the second is gradually building a mental map of the community. This map will contain information about the connections between people, and whether these can be used to advantage as information channels and as a way of giving access to significant resources and influence.

Obviously it is not really feasible for the worker to hold all this personal detail in their memory and it may be advisable to keep records, particularly on private matters, such as the names and contact details of key members of local community groups, or of everyone who has ever expressed an interest in drama, netball, basic literacy classes or whatever. This might be kept on index cards in a box, as lists in the filing cabinet or as a computer database, and it is essential to comply with the Data Protection and Freedom of Information Acts. The important things to consider are issues of confidentiality and ensuring access to the information for those who have a legitimate use for it. It is also vital to keep this information up-to-date and relevant to changing circumstances.

A mental map is different from a community profile, which is often more concerned with hard facts and fellow professionals' views. The 'network knowledge' developed by the community worker is inevitably more dynamic, evolving as the pattern of relationships and circumstances between people shifts and changes. It includes the presence and identity of the community worker *themselves*. The map needs constant updating and revision as new links are informed and old ones dissolve.

Importance of good relationships across the whole community

It is clear that important tools for the community networker include a good memory and an ability to get on well with a variety of people. Community workers need to be versatile in how they communicate and behave in different situations, adapting language and style according to who else is part of the conversation or meeting. Much networking is fairly pragmatic and hidden in the 'nooks and crannies' of the community worker's planned work programme. It involves maintaining open relationships with people and being prepared to initiate new ones.

Community workers must be alert to some contradictions in the use of networking. Networks often operate as exclusive clubs whose membership is restricted to those with certain characteristics or social positions. Informal and personal connections with other individuals are used to exchange information and this may give an advantage to those 'in the know'. In order to maintain a degree of equality of opportunity, the community worker must keep in mind a checklist of individuals and organisations they would make a positive effort to keep informed and involved. For example, it is important to make sure that when schools are sent publicity material about holiday play schemes, the same information is also sent to any segregated schools, which disabled children from the area may attend. Otherwise they may not hear about the play opportunities available in their local neighbourhood.

Community development workers should ensure that, as professionals, they cultivate those relationships that are not part of their own social networks. It is useful to take part in events where they can get to know people they might not normally meet, or who are marginalised by mainstream organisations.

Community workers should also educate themselves about a range of cultures and issues that influence the lives of people with whom they are working. Attention to current affairs, as seen from the perspective of different sections of the population, will enable workers to hold meaningful conversations about issues and events that are relevant to members of different communities and so build up relationships based on mutual respect and concern.

Community brokerage and bridge building

Community workers are frequently instrumental in playing a brokerage role by introducing people to each other and suggesting the possible usefulness of the connection. An example might be: 'Jatinder, this is Kevin. He's interested in getting something done about the swings in the playground, and he knows Liz who works in the Parks Department. Perhaps he might be able to help in your campaign group.' Often, the community worker simply gives information but leaves it up to people themselves to decide whether they get in touch with one another. If this is the case, it is important to be aware that people sometimes find it hard to make contact with a stranger (especially one in an official position) and it may be useful to follow up the suggestion at a later date, to check if any further encouragement is needed.

Creating opportunities for networking

Events such as conferences and training workshops can be ideal occasions for sharing ideas and building contacts. It is often difficult in such forums for people to get to know one another and identify potential connections.

Various tactics can be adopted to make it easier for people to approach one another outside the formal sessions and begin to exchange ideas and information. Wearing name badges, and introductions or 'ice-breakers' at the beginning of any gathering will ensure that people have at least some information about fellow participants, but care needs to be taken to ensure that people with mobility, sensory or mental difficulties are able to take part. Unstructured 'socialising space' at events is also helpful in creating informal, open-ended opportunities for people to make their own connections. It can be useful during the introductions for people to give some personal information in addition to their name, such as where they come from, which group they represent or any other interests.

The community worker, rather like a good host, can be proactive in introducing people to each other who might have something in common or encouraging shy people to mingle. Business cards are increasingly popular, even amongst community workers, and are an easy way of giving someone your name and contact details for future reference. It is also useful to provide conference participants with an attendance list so that people can follow up conversations after the formal event.

Informal occasions offer ideal opportunities for networking, and community work approaches can maximise their potential of these by ensuring that a wide diversity of people is invited. Social activities, such as community festivals or trips, provide plenty of excuses for people who might not otherwise talk to one another to strike up a conversation and discover what they can offer to each other and the wider community. The rationale behind many a community building is not simply to provide a venue for different activities, but to create possibilities for people with different interests and diverse backgrounds to meet in a safe, neutral and communal setting. Indeed, this is an explicit aspect of the function of many settlements and social action centres.

Appropriate, accessible and affordable positive action

It is important to acknowledge the limitations of networking and to recognise when other, perhaps more formal, structures are appropriate. As mentioned earlier, flexible, relatively structureless forms of organisation are vulnerable to pressures both from within and outside the membership. People involved in networks need to be aware of these influences and develop policies or procedures which actively promote equality of opportunity and access. Anti-discriminatory strategies should be incorporated and positive action measures taken wherever resources permit. Network organisers must be vigilant and pro-active in ensuring that the community development principles of full **access**, equal **rights** and mutual **support** are fully integrated into every aspect of the organisation.

Sometimes, however, this is not enough to ensure inclusive participation, so deliberate steps need to be taken to set up connections between people. There are many factors that militate against relationships forming, some created through practical barriers, others by social and psychological factors, such as prejudice and stereotyping. Where necessary, facilitated communication, signing, translators and interpreters should be used, and information made available in whatever languages are required. The atmosphere and culture of the setting can seem exclusive or intimidating to certain sections of the community, and this will almost certainly discourage the participation or interaction of those people who do not feel comfortable or welcome.

Challenging the inequalities and prejudices that exist in every community is a major and fundamental aspect of positive networking. The rest of this section includes some suggestions for how to organise meetings and events to encourage networking and allow participation for anyone who is interested.

Particular attention should be paid to enabling children and young people to become integrated into networks, especially at neighbourhood level. Their interests, enthusiasms and concerns form a vital ingredient in developing joint activities and local campaigns. Their contribution to community life is often marginalised or sentimentalised. In order to achieve their true potential, network development needs to recognise and encourage the links that children and young people have with each other, and their diversity of relationships with a range of adults in the community. For children and young people to feel empowered to participate in networks, it may be necessary to make special arrangements to facilitate their attendance at meetings and allow their voices to be fully heard in decision-making (see Henderson, 1995). There has, in recent years, been an increase in the use of mentors to support young people, who can also act as advocates and role models where needed.

Communication

Networking occurs as much through chance conversations as through the written word. It is important for the community development worker to be an active listener and communicator. It is easy to make false assumptions about another person's agenda, and the worker should be sensitive to the feelings and potential implications behind what someone is saying. Learning to 'hear the silences' is also important – which voices are not speaking out and what significant or contentious issues are not being raised? Asking questions and expressing enthusiasm or concern for the subject will encourage the other person to speak more, and allow the community worker to clarify their interest and elicit more facts and/or opinions. Information should be presented in a way that is both accessible and relevant. Written documents should be in plain English, avoiding where possible the use of jargon, and all abbreviations should be fully explained within the text. Ideally, translations of these documents should be available in the first language of all potential participants, for example minority ethnic languages, large print, video-taped British Sign Language, audio tape and Braille. Wherever feasible, background material needed for a discussion should be circulated to potential participants in advance of meetings to allow time for translation, clarification and consultation. This would also ensure that members were sufficiently prepared to contribute fully to the debate and to feel confident that they were familiar with the views of those they are representing.

Within meetings, communication between participants may need to be formally facilitated and assisted. Someone, usually the chair, should take responsibility for ensuring that contributions are clearly articulated and understood. This may involve communication through interpreters or personal assistants and extra time needs to be allowed for this in the flow of the debate. Multiple conversations make interpretation virtually impossible and it is therefore vital that some degree of formality is maintained for plenary sessions and workshop discussions.

Venues

The venue must be fully accessible in every sense. It should be easy to get to by public transport and with good car parking facilities. If this is not the case, then parking spaces for people with mobility impairments should be reserved near the entrance, close to dropped kerbs. Wheelchair users should have level or ramped access, with lifts to upper floors, and there should be accessible toilets within easy reach of the meeting place. Rooms being used should be clearly signposted, warm and comfortable. A smoky atmosphere can make it impossible for people with asthma and other respiratory problems to attend. If possible, a quiet space should be set aside for those who need a rest or a break from the proceedings for prayer or simply to collect their thoughts.

Facilities and assistance should be readily available for people with any kind of special requirements. Induction loops may be permanently fitted or a mobile version used. Background noise should be kept to a minimum, as this is very distracting for all participants and disabling for people with hearing impairments. Interpreters, advocates and personal assistants should be properly trained and paid.

The conduct of meetings

Meetings provide an important forum for exchanging information and influencing decision-making. If networks are to sustain a commitment to openness and participatory democracy, meetings must be conducted in an inclusive way. Sufficient advance notice should be given to allow people to make arrangements to attend, and once the date and time are fixed they should not be altered at the last minute, even by having the meeting finish earlier than expected. This is because people who are reliant on others for their transport need to make their arrangements in advance and should be able to keep to them.

If meetings are to last for more than about two hours, include breaks so that people can rest, regain their concentration and take some refreshment. This is particularly important if interpreters are being used, and in any case, not all participants will have the stamina or the inclination to be in a meeting for this length of time.

The language and style of discussion should encourage participation. People should be asked to speak as clearly as they can and avoid language that is obscure or offensive to other participants. Nearly everyone will have ideas or information to share, and ways should be found to facilitate input from anyone who wishes to contribute. Breaking up into smaller groups or pairs can encourage people to speak their mind, as can the use of methods such as brainstorming or even role play. People should be asked to identify themselves when speaking, so that they can be contacted afterwards by anyone who is interested in talking further with them.

Disagreements will be inevitable within groups of such diversity, but should be handled in a way that acknowledges strong emotions and beliefs, without deteriorating into personal attacks and acrimony. The facilitator must be able and willing to challenge inappropriate behaviour and language, and to offer support for those who may find such situations daunting.

The timing of meetings will be influential in determining who can attend. Daytime meetings will help ensure attendance from paid workers, but will deter those volunteers who are active in community groups at weekends or evenings, but have a day-time job or attend school. Evening meetings cause problems in relation to transport and people's sense of safety, especially in poorly lit or high crime neighbourhoods. Childcare should be provided via a crèche or payments for childminding or evening babysitting. Expenses should also be available to enable carers who have responsibility for adult dependents. It may be a good idea to alternate the times and days of meetings, but this does run the risk of causing confusion and a loss of continuity.

Overcoming obstacles to networking

Many of these suggestions require resources and some will be quite expensive or difficult to implement. Nevertheless, they highlight factors that can hinder participation by many people in mainstream community development networks and consultation procedures. Wherever possible funding should be made available to introduce positive action measures; at the very least, effort needs to be made to counter some of these barriers and enable people to network with one another on equal terms. Networking that neglects community development values is likely to be both ineffectual and unethical. Bad networking occurs when it is simply promoting personal interests or is used (deliberately or otherwise) to exclude certain people or sections of the population from a legitimate role in decision-making. The term 'meta-networking' is just a new, rather clumsy piece of jargon. It is intended to convey the community development worker's responsibility in *helping others* to make links that might otherwise be problematic.

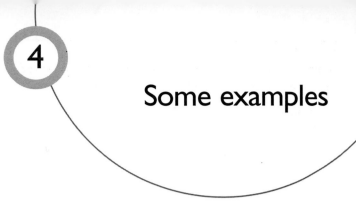

Some examples

Networks and networking allow people to gain greater control over their lives. By broadening and enriching existing connections among people operating within and around a particular community or issue, networking enables people to help themselves and tackle some of the problems they and others experience. Informal social networks are vital to the proper functioning of communities, providing an essential (but largely invisible) part of the community's capacity to organise collective action and engage with partnership bodies. The more diverse and inclusive these networks, the better the flow of information, resources and influence.

Networking has been effective in:

- setting up support mechanisms
- lobbying for policy changes
- providing forums for debate and information exchange, and
- developing community-based services based on mutual aid and respect.

There is today great interest in the network as an organisational form that has the potential to promote innovation in service delivery. People involved in community development recognise the value of networking and have set up a variety of networks for practitioners and others involved in working with communities. The degree of organisation underpinning networks can range from formal to informal. Networks' levels of activity also vary – some lie dormant until needed for a specific purpose, whilst others are more proactive in raising issues and organising events. Networks can be quite formally structured, with clear membership criteria and a stated purpose. This is often the case when networks have evolved to a stage where they employ workers or manage resources, and in such instances are usually referred to as partnerships. Other networks operate more informally as loose associations of like-minded people. Their lack of rules and regulations allow them to respond more flexibly to participants' changing needs and interests. Most networks operate somewhere between these extremes, with broad aims and flexible procedures, based on shared values and good interpersonal relationships.

Practitioners create or become involved in community development-based networks for four main reasons. Networks:

- provide mutual support through face-to-face interaction
- create opportunities for learning and reflection
- act as a mechanism for campaigning and consultation
- allow an exchange of experience that promotes 'good practice' and challenges 'bad practice'.

The following examples illustrate how networks have been effective in setting up support mechanisms, providing forums for debate and information sharing, lobbying for policy changes and mobilising for action. Some networks are geographically based, whilst others have a specific focus or interest.

Active Partners

One example of a formal network is Active Partners, which was formed in 1998 after concern was expressed about local communities' lack of involvement in community regeneration. A group of regional bodies, including the regional development agency Yorkshire Forward, the Churches Regional Commission, Yorkshire and the Humber Regional Forum and Yorkshire and Humber Assembly, worked with communities across the region to develop a set of benchmarks to measure the effectiveness of community involvement. The Active Partners Unit promotes best practice in community involvement by supporting initiatives to use the benchmarks and sharing learning regionally through events and resources.

The Unit has set up the Active Partners Network, which now has over 300 members, including regeneration and planning officers, community activists and local development agencies. Its aim is to promote community participation in regeneration by helping local people to get more involved by challenging regeneration schemes and partnerships to improve their communication with the local community. The network supports any partnership, project and scheme with a remit around community participation and which is involved in the regeneration of disadvantaged communities. Network members have access to an information service, an advice line and resources including a newsletter, plus training opportunities to learn 'how to' and 'how not to' do community participation, using the benchmarking model. It uses the internet and events to network and so build alliances with partners across the region.

Ubuntu[1]

Ubuntu is a national network of black and minority ethnic (BME) practitioners from across the UK who work or have an interest in promoting and delivering community development work from a black perspective. It is part of the Federation for Community Development Learning (FDCL) – a network of individuals, groups and organisations involved in community development work and training.

Ubuntu is a place for creating, meeting, sharing and providing support for the benefit of all its members. Black perspectives describes a relationship between people that seeks to enrich the individuals involved through process as well as content. It describes a perspective that challenges beliefs and behaviours that lead to inequalities, disadvantage and loss. It also describes a way of viewing the world that recognises and validates the contributions that BME people make to society as a whole.

The network is supported by a development worker based within the FCDL. It publishes a quarterly newsletter and organises conferences that bring together practitioners from all sectors and from across the UK. The network's main objectives are to: inform and develop BME practitioners by skill sharing across different sectors and disciplines that add to black perspectives of community development learning and training; influence and contribute to policy development by working in partnership with regional, national and other relevant BME groups and networks; and strengthen links between BME infrastructure organisations and networks by supporting networking, skills sharing and training.

Northumberland Community Development Network (NCDN)

NCDN is committed to supporting community development good practice at the local level and using networking to build links between localities, to enable a stronger collective voice across the sub-region, and has therefore developed a working networking model.

---

1   An African concept that expresses the belief that 'people are people through other people'.

NCDN was established in 2002, after wide consultation with individuals and groups from all sectors. In 2003 the Northumberland Community Development Company was formed, to give NCDN the formal status it needed to attract funds and develop its activities.

NCDN works through four task groups that feed into a working group, which is an open meeting for anyone interested in being an active member of the network. Each meeting hears from local community networks and agrees the network programme. The network's formal body, NCDC, has members from different interests within the network, and formally agrees decisions made by the working group. Networking activities take place within each strand of the company's work and task groups.

NCDC manages a growing database of contacts for individuals and organisations working in community development. Communications across the county have been improved as a result of the development of the website, which includes network and general news, feedback on each task group's activities and a focus on each of the six districts within the county. The network has a holistic approach to work.

A major area of activity for the company is providing learning and support to practitioners through community development training. This has included a series of 30-hour introductory courses, run in partnership with local organisations across the county. Next steps are to develop satellite learning and support centres around the county to create better access for local learners and further develop workplace learning for voluntary and community organisations. NCDC has also overseen the development of an action learning scheme.

It is committed to supporting community development good practice at a local level and uses networking to build links between localities in order to develop a stronger collective voice across the county. One example is the Children's Fund commissioning NCDC to work with the children and young people's strategic partnership and young people's equality group.

Community Development and Health Network in Northern Ireland (CDHN)

CDHN was established in 1994 as an umbrella body supporting people and developing healthier communities in Northern Ireland. The membership is open to individuals and organisations from statutory, academic, voluntary and community agencies who share the underpinning ethos and values of the network.

CDHN's vision is to effect change at policy, organisational and practice level, promoting action to redress poverty and inequality in health. It understands health in its broadest sense and believes that a community development approach to health 'recognises the central importance of social support networks. It is a process by which a community defines its own health needs to bring about change. The emphasis is on collective action to redress inequalities and enhance access to health care'.

The network works towards its mission through four strategic aims:

- **Network** – to sustain and extend a significant inter-sectoral membership network that is complementary, democratic, member-led, active and influential.

- **Change** – to provide leadership to promote action on the links between poverty, inequality, community development and health and demonstrate how community development is an appropriate and valid method of supporting action on health inequalities.

- **Practice** – to promote and support creativity, innovation, development, application and understanding of community development and health practice.

- **Organisation** – to sustain and continually develop CDHN as an organisation that both fulfils its responsibilities and delivers its aims efficiently and effectively, offering value for money in ways that contribute to social capital.

CDHN produces a quarterly magazine *A Healthy Debate,* which attempts to chart recent developments in the community development and health field, and also produces a monthly information bulletin *Healthy Bites,* which is distributed to members and contacts across Northern Ireland and the Republic.

Wakefield District Community Network

This district-wide network provides a forum whereby people can express support for community development work by sharing and developing their knowledge and skills. It developed because of the lack of support for community development workers in the district; there was no forum to share good practice and no co-ordinated approach to training and support. The network agreed to encourage networking, arrange regular meetings, provide mutual support and encouragement, identify and provide training, share information, lobby for more resources for communities and actively encourage greater involvement in the distribution and management of local resources.

It then developed 'CODEworks' to act as a representative group of community development workers who promote good practice and encourage a community development approach in strategy and policy development. Due to some managers' lack of understanding of community development work and the absence of professional development programmes, a community development managers group was established with the purpose of sharing good practice and coherent planning of community development work.

It was realised by the network that there was no shared definition of community development and there was a need for a district-wide strategic approach. A community development good practice (CDGP) group was therefore established with two aims: to formulate policy in relation to community development and to develop more strategic working with communities within Wakefield District.

A shared definition and vision was produced, the CDGP group became a formal part of the local strategic partnership and funding was sought for a dedicated post to take work forward. Despite these successes the network experienced difficulties in terms of lack of time for workers and appropriate funding to take initiatives forward.

Shropshire Community Development Network

This is a relatively new network started by a community development worker to support and promote community development. The network defines community development as a way of enabling communities of geography, interest or identity to achieve social change and justice by working collectively in ways which challenge oppression and tackle inequalities.

The network's aim is the development of community development policy and guardianship of community development values and practice standards in Shropshire. It began its activities by mapping community development workers and community projects by arranging visits to projects for network members and sharing practice between community projects and community workers. The network covers the whole of the county and membership is informal, open to anybody who defines themselves as doing community work.

The network's main activities are steering and supporting professional training and development for community workers, identifying the need for and providing community-based training in community development skills and knowledge, co-mentoring between workers, and advocating with statutory and voluntary agencies for community development to be seen as an effective contributor to community cohesion and equality.

Network members meet every two months but mostly communicate through an e-mail-based network. The meetings are structured over a day, with business and networking in the morning and project visits in the afternoon. The meetings are moved around the county to allow others to attend and promote their activities.

Staffordshire and Stoke-on-Trent Community Development Network

The principal aim of this network is to promote and encourage effective community development practice within Staffordshire. The network grew from a number of community development events organised by the community council of Staffordshire and funded by the Countryside Agency. Several community development workers from urban and rural backgrounds attended workshop-based sessions to gauge the support for a network.

Recommendations from these events included establishing more support and joined-up action for community development workers, linked in to existing partnerships. A plan of action was agreed, and highlighted priorities included networking for support and mutual benefit, both informally via e-mail and formally through mentor or 'buddy' systems. Links were also established with local organisations such as the Staffordshire Training Consortium and Staffordshire Partnership.

Meetings are held quarterly in order to continue practice sharing and networking. They include some formal business but mainly facilitate informal sharing of ideas and experiences. Each meeting has a different focus and is relevant to a broad range of community development workers and practitioners. The network has produced promotional literature (an information pack containing terms of reference, definitions and an action plan) and developed a website, and maintains a members' contact database.

Stockton-on-Tees Community Development Workers Network

This network was formed in September 2003. It began with a large meeting of community development workers from across the borough discussing ways to share ideas, identify community assets and strengths, and develop greater sustainability.

The group agreed that a partnership arrangement or network would be the best way to move these objectives forward.

The purpose of the network is to promote the achievements and success of community development work in Stockton, share community development practice and projects across the borough, create education and training opportunities for development workers, and develop a more sustainable impact for community development projects.

The network is for people who work in and with communities in Stockton and those who adopt a community development approach in their service. People join the network to be recognised and valued, to meet others with similar interests in projects, to develop opportunities for joint working, and to support others who are working in isolation and areas of disadvantage.

The network operates through quarterly members' meetings, via the community development workers' website, through e-mails and through subgroup meetings. The subgroups include training and education, funding and resources, communication, and mapping community development provision.

The focus of the network is centred on community development workers who have front-line experience of working in and with communities. It is not intended to be a replacement for the community-based and capacity building networks in the borough, but its emphasis is related to community-based practice and projects rather than an agency or public involvement approach. The network is looking to support community development workers by advancing professional growth through community development training and conferences.

Community Development Exchange (CDX)

CDX is the UK membership organisation for community development practitioners. Its mission is to be a strong and effective voice for community development. It is a membership-led organisation, aiming to bring about positive changes towards social justice and equality by using and promoting the values and approaches of community development. It works to ensure that community development is recognised as a powerful way of tackling inequality and achieving social justice.

The membership base is diverse and comes from all sectors, including local authorities, policymakers, academics, non-profit organisations, voluntary and community organisations, independent researchers and trainers and grassroots community workers, throughout the four countries of the UK. Members represent a range of interest, experience and perspectives while sharing a belief that a clear set of values and commitments should be at the heart of developing active and sustainable communities.

CDX acts a catalyst for change by sharing information, experience and practice, including resources, through a variety of means including conferences, research, newsletters, websites and, more significantly, networking the networks. For example, it has a networking development fund to help local and specialist networks to share information and expertise. People can have access to research and policy information from the UK-wide community worker survey.

CDX has developed the strategic framework for community development – a working tool to promote community development work and practice. It has also developed a networking resource pack to help networks develop their aims and objectives. CDX's own database and newsletter provide information and contact names and addresses for a huge variety of network-type organisations across the UK. The organisation brings together practitioners who are involved in regional, national and specialist networks, through mini conferences. These gatherings provide valuable opportunities for community development workers to meet and work with others to preserve and promote the core aims and values of community development. CDX is currently supporting the development of two networks, Community Development Cymru and Scottish Community Development Network.

Community Development Cymru (CDC)

CDC is an independent all-Wales, member-led organisation and network of networks. It aims to develop a common understanding of the values and practice of community development by promoting it at all levels as a collective voice in community development. It also aims to strengthen support for community development workers and community development and plays an active role in the advancement of standards in community development practice.

Membership is open to anyone involved in or with an interest and commitment to community development, whether paid or non-paid, particularly from community networks, co-operatives and community groups. The network's main priority is to promote the community development process across all sectors and support the development of local community development networks.

Scottish Community Development Network (SCDN)

SCDN is a membership-led organisation for community workers, paid or unpaid, full or part-time, from the community, voluntary or public sectors, who support the principles and practice of community development. The network was formally constituted in 1999.

SCDN works with its members through organising seminars, producing information, and providing opportunities to comment on consultations and forums for discussion and debate on community development issues. The network's strategic aim is to strengthen the collective voice for community development in Scotland and strengthen links with other organisations that work with communities.

Community development workers' networks

In addition to the formal networks described above, community development workers can use their own networks to help in organising major events and joint projects. Networking from one contact to the next is one way of gaining access to vital information and resources. It is also a way of eliciting 'off the record' opinions from unattributable sources in local authorities or other official institutions. Community workers will deliberately use their reputation and links with other colleagues to identify and contact someone who can help out with a particular task or to spread the word about a new initiative.

Community development workers often use their knowledge of people, groups and organisations and the connections between them to carry out their work. Being on friendly terms with the local councillor may indirectly give access to the chair of an important committee or even the ruling party group, whose policies can be swayed for community benefit. Networking is an effective method for reaching people in the community with whom the worker has no direct relationship, but who can be tracked down through known or suspected intermediary contacts. Community networks provide important mechanisms for ensuring that community representatives are supported and held accountable for their work on partnership boards.

Other types of networks

Networks offer ways in which individuals from a cross-section of organisations can work together towards a specific purpose. They provide opportunities for people working around a common theme to come together to share experience and develop collective strategies for challenging inequalities and discrimination. Sometimes networks have a general goal, attracting membership purely on the basis of a shared identity or experience of oppression. A network can often provide the springboard to setting up a consultative group or working party that draws on a number of perspectives and different experiences. Networks as campaigning organisations can be effective in developing a collective view in order to strengthen an argument for social or political change without necessarily jeopardising member groups' autonomy or charitable status.

Networks can often be specifically established to cross boundaries. Such boundaries might be expressed in the division between voluntary and statutory sectors, or between communities separated by ideological or religious differences. Networking enables people to find common ground, build trust and create alliances for collective action.

The examples in this section illustrate various ways in which networking and different forms of networks are used to further the aims of community development. They differ in terms of membership and the degree of formal structure, but have one aspect in common:

All are organised to enable individual participants to make connections with one another without the necessity for meetings or rigid procedures.

Regardless of whether they call themselves forums, coalitions or something else, network-type organisations are distinguished from other forms of association by this characteristic. In particular, if there is centralised mechanism such as a secretariat group, this should do no more than facilitate or coordinate. Attempts to control or limit the flow of information and ideas through the web of connections should be resisted. Initiatives involving many organisations that do not allow this multiple and uncoordinated interaction to occur are not true networks. It is important to recognise that the essential features of a network are the informal cross-connections, rather than any particular word used in its title.

However, networks are not suited to all purposes. Where control, predictability or accountability is important, they might complement rather than replace more hierarchical arrangements. Helping a network to develop into an organisation, without losing the key networking attributes is a vital task for community development workers; one which sometimes requires great delicacy and diplomacy.

Development issues for the future

Valuing and evaluating networks

Although networking has always formed part of community development practice, it is only in the last decade or so that it has been acknowledged as an explicit method of community development. Strengthening community networks builds capacity and enables communities to engage more effectively with public decision-making processes. In some respects, networking and meta-networking can be seen as essential to the work of developing 'community' (Gilchrist, 2004b). Government has recognised this in its recently published report *Firm Foundations* (CRU, 2004). It recommends that every area should have some kind of 'hub' or 'anchor' organisation that community members can use to support their activities and networking. **Relationships** and **information** are the principal assets used by community workers in developing community initiatives and encouraging partnership between different sectors. Networking is a method of laying down a foundation for this work, and should be valued as an essential aspect of community development.

Networks should therefore be evaluated against both the **processes** of community development and **specific goals**, such as improved services, structures or policy developments. However, because it is sometimes difficult to claim tangible or predictable outcomes from networking, its value is often underestimated by managers and funders. The current emphasis on targets and performance indicators for evaluating community development work can jeopardise the serendipitous nature of networking, which is a combination of good fortune and strategic planning. The evaluation of networking must therefore be viewed in relation to **longer-term outcomes**, rather than the achievement of immediate and direct changes or simplistic output measures. The following recommendations affirm that networking is an **investment** in future developments, even though these may not yet be planned or even envisaged.

Time and training

Those who are responsible for managing and funding community development should recognise that time and skills are needed for developing networks, and allow for this in the work programmes of the workers they employ or supervise. Competence and understanding of networking is valuable and can be enhanced through training. Community workers should be encouraged to put time and effort into developing and sustaining networks, both in terms of their own contacts and in terms of community capacity building. The impact of this on their work as a whole can be regularly evaluated. Helping workers to understand how their work is supported through networks of personal contacts, professional relationships and chance conversations will encourage them to appreciate and build on these aspects of community involvement. Most networks are self-organising and depend on their members having the time and inclination to undertake any necessary tasks. Community development workers have a special responsibility to promote and contribute to this practice by making sure that these processes are inclusive and proactive in combating inequalities. Support for, and participation in, networks should be seen as an essential rather than an optional part of the community work role, and this aspect of the job should be protected, even though the outcomes are often indirect, unpredictable or delayed.

Resourcing the infrastructure

Many networks face problems in obtaining adequate resourcing for their basic functions. Public money, such as that channelled through the Change Up funds, usually requires that organisations are properly constituted with formal accounting procedures in place. Sometimes networks just need time and money to support members' involvement in various activities. This function can be undermined or distorted if decision-making structures become too cumbersome or centralised. This could include the cost of meeting rooms, mailings, administrative expenses and the positive action measures referred to in Section 3. Many networks are being established on the basis of directories and computer-held databases. Information technology can be extremely useful in helping people to contact and stay in touch with one another, but only if any such applications are available in ways that are managed and understood by the users. A 'digital divide' has emerged in recent years between those who have easy access to the internet (for websites, e-mailings and chat forums) and those who are reliant on more traditional means of communication, such as word of mouth or the post. However, we have also seen the rise of information overload brought about by 'spamming' of unsolicited messages and excessive 'list' mailings.

Whilst informal networks function well without organisational structures, formal networks certainly need some degree of co-ordination if they are to survive and be effective. For some networks, servicing can be done by members taking it in turns to convene and facilitate meetings or send out mailings. This has the advantage that skills and power are shared as widely as possible across the whole group and a range of perspectives is allowed to influence the network. Alternatively, one person can provide the secretariat or servicing function, who might be elected from within the membership or appointed to a paid position from outside. This person would be the main point of contact for members and other agencies, which can help solve the problem of how prospective members and 'outsiders' can make initial contact with the network.

Resources should be made available to support networks' infrastructures. Intermediary bodies, such as rural community councils, councils for voluntary service or local 'anchor' organisations, can provide valuable administrative support for organisational tasks such as mailings, and convening and servicing meetings. They can also act as a contact address for correspondence or enquiries. A small amount of funding for co-ordination or administration can be a helpful and cost-effective means of enabling a network to develop its core structure and identity.

Democratic procedures are necessary to ensure the accountability of the central co-ordinating figure or group. To some extent these people will inevitably have to exercise some discretion (and therefore influence) over which decisions are taken by the whole organisation, and what or how information is disseminated to members. Sometimes the need for a paid co-coordinator can be a sign that the organisation is in transition from being a network (with power and contacts relatively equally distributed across the membership) to becoming a different kind of association, with the beginnings of a hierarchical structure and centralised administration. This needs to be acknowledged, and a clear collective decision made about whether (and how) the network will move on to the next stage of its evolution.

Clarity around aims and functions of networks

As networks grow beyond a certain optimal size, they can become elitist, unwieldy and even discriminatory. When it is no longer possible for members to be easily in touch with one another, mechanisms may need to be introduced to ensure that internal communication is not restricted to an unrepresentative core group.

Similarly, decision-making may need to be formalised to prevent domination by a centralised clique. Accountability is a fragile commodity in any organisation, and networks that lack adequate democratic structures find themselves especially vulnerable to distortion and takeovers. Trust between network members is an important ingredient in helping such organisations function without too many formal procedures.

In this respect, clarity around roles, responsibilities and democratic procedures will minimise these possibilities. But it may also detract from what is the essence and value of a network-type association, namely its flexibility and openness. A clear statement of aims and values, with a limited and simple set of objectives, may suffice as a constitution which all members can understand and subscribe to. Complications seem to arise if the objectives are either too vague or too detailed. Controversy or unrealistic expectations tend to put pressure on what can be a rather flimsy framework. If greater levels of collaboration and representation are required, then a different form of organisation is probably needed. This may involve setting up a new organisation alongside the network, or it may require the network itself to evolve into a more rigid, centrally-organised structure.

Further research possibilities

Although the process of networking may seem a very familiar concept to many people involved in community development, there has been little investigation of what actually happens as a result of networking. Research into the networking practice of community workers indicated that many do indeed make and use informal connections in the course of their work and that their networking has significant outcomes in terms of stronger communities and better partnership working (Gilchrist, 2001; 2004b). A systematic investigation of the impact of community initiatives and community development work on networks in action would provide evidence of how networking can be correlated with various policy outcomes and government programmes, as well as generally supporting informal co-operation and communication.

Conclusions

The unique contribution of networks to community development reflects the informal and often invisible nature of this method of community work. It is an organic approach, which creates and nurtures connections between people without a pre-conceived purpose. Networking allows experience, expertise and enthusiasm to cross boundaries, thus challenging the barriers that exist between organisations and different sections of society.

The release of this potential relies as much on the imagination and personal contacts of community development workers, as on the establishment of formal structures. As with so many aspects of community work, it is a highly skilled, little recognised, but increasingly effective strategy for community development, which deserves more recognition and support. This booklet has highlighted the main features of networking, and illustrates how it is used for community development. A growing awareness of the value of this approach can only enhance the impact and value of community development in creating a more equal and democratic society.

Resources for further networking

Action with Communities in Rural England (ACRE)
Somerford Court
Somerford Road
Cirencester
Gloucestershire GL7 1TW
Tel: 01285 65 3477
E-mail: acre@acre.org.uk
Internet: www.acre.org.uk

A national charity whose purpose is to support sustainable rural community development. It provides a national platform for its founder member rural community councils, other bodies and individuals who work at local, county, regional and national levels to alleviate rural disadvantage in England.

ADEPT Community Development Agency
3 Market Way
Coventry CV1 1DF
Tel: 024 7623 0606
E-mail: info@adept.org.uk
Internet: www.adept.org.uk

Provides community development, regeneration apprenticeship programmes, accredited or bespoke community work training, research and consultancy services. Client groups include local partnerships, local authorities, voluntary organisations, community development agencies and community groups and CENs.

Association of Community Workers (ACW)
Balliol Youth and Community Centre
Longbenton Methodist Church
Chesters Avenue
Newcastle NE12 8QP
Tel: 0191 215 1880
E-mail: leslieleach@acw1.fsbusiness.co.uk

A national membership organisation made up of individuals and community workers. Produces a monthly bulletin with discussion papers – Talking Point – and organises an annual conference. Represents community work on a number of consultative committees and is able to put members in touch with one another on a basis of shared interests.

Black and Ethnic Minorities Infrastructure in Scotland (BEMIS)
The Mansfield Traquair Centre
15 Mansfield Place
Edinburgh EH3 6BB

Tel: 0131 474 8045
Fax: 0131 474 2790
E-mail: mail@bemis.org.uk
Internet: www.bemis.org.uk

The national umbrella body supporting the development of the black and minority ethnic (BME) voluntary sector throughout Scotland. BEMIS provides a voice and works to ensure capacity building for the sector and the communities it. Also provides a platform to work in partnership with the public and private sectors on issues that relate to BME communities, which promote the value of diversity, equality and social justice for all.

Black Information Link
(1990 Trust – BIL)
Suite 12, Winchester House
9 Cranmer Road
London SW9 6EJ
Tel: 020 7582 1990
E-mail: blink1990@blink.org.uk

The Trust was set up to work on issues facing BME people living in Britain, using a grassroots black perspective. It provides information, advice, research and technical support to black community organisations. It sees networking as a principle that is both fundamental to black community development and essential for sustaining the work of black organisations across Britain.

British Association of Settlements
and Social Action Centres (bassac)
33 Corsham Street
London N1 6DR
Tel: 0845 241 0375
E-mail: info@bassac.org.uk
Internet: www.bassac.org.uk

bassac is a membership organisation that represents and supports a national network of organisations that provide services and community development support and host smaller community initiatives. Located in areas of deprivation, they strengthen neighbourhoods and increase opportunities for local people.

Churches' Community Work
Alliance (CCWA)
St Chad's College
North Bailey
Durham DH1 3RH
Tel: 0191 334 3346
Fax: 0191 334 3371
Mobile: 07866 80 4460
E-mail: info@ccwa.org.uk
Internet: www.ccwa.org.uk

Promotes and supports church-related community development work across the UK and the Republic of Ireland.

Community Development and
Health Network (CDHN)
30a Mill Street
Newry BT34 1EY
Tel: 028 3026 4606
E-mail: kathymcardle@cdhn.org
Internet: www.cdhn.org

A voluntary membership organisation committed to promoting and supporting action on health issues. The Network understands health in its broadest context and works toward addressing all the factors affecting health.

Community Development Foundation (CDF)

Unit 5, Angel Gate
320–326 City Road
London EC1V 2PT
Tel: 020 7226 5375
Fax: 020 7704 0313
E-mail: info@cdf.org.uk
Internet: www.cdf.org.uk

A charity and non-departmental public body which works through local action projects and networks; development and best practice; research, evaluation and policy analysis; consultancy and training; conferences and seminars; information and publications.

Community Matters

12–20 Baron Street
London N1 9LL
Tel: 020 7837 7887
E-mail: communitymatters@
communitymatters.org.uk
Internet: www.communitymatters.org.uk

Plays a key role in promoting and supporting action by ordinary people in response to social, educational and recreational needs in their neighbourhoods and communities.

Community Practitioners and Health Visitors Association (CPHVA)

33–37 Moreland Street
London EC1V 8HA
Tel: 020 7780 4000
E-mail: infocphva@amicustheunion.org
Internet: www.msfcphva.org

CPHVA is a section within the trade union Amicus. It is a UK professional body representing registered nurses and health visitors working in a primary or community health setting. Includes a community development special interest group, which aims to provide networks and disseminate good practice information.

Community Work Education and Training Network (CWETN)

Philip House
123–137 York Street
Belfast BT15 1AB
Tel: 028 9023 2618
E-mail: info@cwetn.org
Internet: www.cwetn.org

CWETN's mission is to network organisations that promote community development learning, which creates empowered and articulate communities.

Consortium of Lesbian, Gay, Bisexual and Transgendered Voluntary and Community Organisations

Unit J414
Tower Bridge Business Complex
100 Clements Road
London SE16 4DG
Tel: 020 7064 8383

Fax: 020 7064 8283
E-mail: admin@lgbtconsortium.org.uk
Internet: www.lgbtconsortium.org.uk

A membership network of over 400 groups working in lesbian, gay and bisexual (LGB) communities around the UK.

The Council of Ethnic Minority Voluntary Sector Organisations (CEMVO)

Boardman House
64 The Broadway
London E15 1NG
Tel: 0208 432 0000 or freephone 0800 652 0390 for further information
E-mail: info@emf-cemvo.co.uk
Internet: www.ethnicminorityfund.co.uk

Aims to strengthen and support the ethnic minority voluntary sector and influence policy debates by articulating the specific needs of disadvantaged communities in the UK.

Development Trusts Association

London Regional Office
1st Floor, 3 Bondway
London SW8 1SJ
Tel: 0845 458 8138
Fax: 0845 458 8337
E-mail: r.jones@dta.org.uk
Internet: www.dta.org.uk

The community based regeneration network 'creating wealth in communities and keeping it there'.

FbRN UK

Kensington Charity Centre
4th Floor, Charles House
375 Kensington High Street
London W14 8QH
Tel: 020 7471 6792
E-mail: fbrnuk@aol.com
Internet: www.fbrn.org.uk

FbRN was established in 2002 by and for regeneration practitioners who identify with faith traditions. It aims to enable faith-based practitioners to learn and gain inspiration from each other, demonstrate the benefit of cross-faith collaboration and co-operation while promoting diversity, provide an interface between the various levels of decision making, and build a shared and evolving learning culture.

Federation for Community Development Learning (FCDL)

4th Floor, Furnival House
48 Furnival Gate
Sheffield S1 4QP
Tel: 0114 273 9391
E-mail: info@fcdl.org.uk
Internet: www.fcdl.org.uk

The UK membership network for those with an interest in community development learning and training. (Formerly known as the Federation of Community Work Training Groups.) FCDL encourages good practice by exchanging ideas, through regular publications and through regional and national events.

International Association for Community Development
PO Box 23680
Edinburgh EH6 6XX
Tel: 0131 554 9977
E-mail: info@iacdglobal.org
Internet: www.iacdglobal.org

An international not-for-profit, non-government organisation committed to building a global network of people and organisations working toward social justice through community development.

National Association of Councils for Voluntary Service (NACVS)
177 Arundel Street
Sheffield S1 2NU
Tel: 0114 278 6636
E-mail: nacvs@nacvs.org.uk
Internet: www.nacvs.org.uk

A network of councils for voluntary service (CVS) and other local voluntary and community infrastructure organisations throughout England. It helps to promote voluntary and community action by supporting member CVS and by acting as a national voice for the local voluntary and community sector.

NCVO
Regent's Wharf
8 All Saints Street
London N1 9RL
Tel: 020 7713 6161
E-mail: ncvo@ncvo-vol.org.uk
Internet: www.ncvo-vol.org.uk

The umbrella body for the voluntary sector in England, with members ranging from large national bodies to community groups, volunteer bureaux, and development agencies working at local level. Works mainly as a lobbying and information service for the sector.

Northern Ireland Council for Voluntary Action (NICVA)
61 Duncairn Gardens
Belfast BT15 2GB
Tel: 028 9087 7777
E-mail: info@nicva.org
Internet: www.nicva.org

The umbrella body for voluntary, community and charitable groups in Northern Ireland. Provides affiliated members with information, advice and training on a range of issues, from management consultancy and finance, through to policy development and lobbying. NICVA adopts a community development approach and empowers local communities to pursue their own needs and agendas.

Quest Trust
1 Belmont
Landsdown Road
Bath BA1 5DZ
Tel: 01225 46 6307
E-mail: simonbuxton@questtrust.co.uk
Internet: www.quest-net.org

Aims to support local activists improving the quality of life in their communities by enabling people to share information and ideas about successful economic and social regeneration effectively, in particular to promote and encourage resident-led, local solutions.

Ubuntu
Federation for Community Development Learning
4th Floor, Furnival House
48 Furnival Gate
Sheffield S1 4QP
Tel: 0114 273 9391
E-mail: carol@fcdl.org.uk
Internet: www.fcdl.org.uk

A collective of individual black and minority ethnic practitioners and activists, networks and groups who share an interest in promoting and delivering learning from black perspectives on community development work. Ubuntu is a special interest group of the Federation for Community Development Learning (FCDL).

Urban Forum
70 Cowcross Street
London EC1M 6EJ
Tel: 020 7253 4816
Fax: 020 7253 4817
E-mail: info@urbanforum.org.uk
Internet: www.urbanforum.org.uk

An umbrella body for community and voluntary groups with interests in urban and regional policy, especially regeneration. It was set up in 1994 as the national voluntary organisation through which local and central government could relate to the community and voluntary sectors on such issues. It aims to provide a strong voluntary sector voice on urban and regional policy and the promotion of sustainable regeneration initiatives.

National and regional community development networks

Community Development Cymru (CDC)
Plas Dolerw
Milford Road
Newtown
Powys SY16 2EH
Tel & Fax : 01686 62 7377
E-mail: admin@cdc.cymru.org
Internet: www.cdc.cymru.org

Membership organisation promoting community development throughout Wales.

CDNE (Community Development North East)
E-mail: cdne@hotmail.com
Internet: www.cdne.org.uk

A new network to assist community development practitioners and policy-makers from all sectors, paid and unpaid, to work together to develop and promote community development throughout the North East.

Community Development South East
30 Mead End Road
Denmead
Waterlooville
Hampshire PO7 6PZ
Tel: 02392 35 6936
E-mail: equal.voices@ntlworld.com
Internet: www.cdse.org.uk

New South East regional community development network. The role of the network is to promote best practice, improve training provision, influence regional policy, spread understanding of what community development is all about.

The Scottish Community Development Centre
Suite 329
Baltic Chambers
50 Wellington Street
Glasgow G2 6HJ
Tel: 0141 248 1924
E-mail: info@scdc.org.uk
Internet: www.scdc.org.uk

The Scottish Community Development Centre – the designated National Development Centre for community development in Scotland – is an innovative partnership between the Community Development Foundation (a UK non-departmental public body funded by government to support community development) and the University of Glasgow.

Scottish Community Development Network (SCDN)
PO Box 26792
Glasgow G4 7AF
E-mail: info@scdn.org.uk
Internet: www.scdn.org.uk

A member-led organisation 'supporting people who support communities in Scotland' for community workers/ community development workers, paid or unpaid, full or part-time, from the community, voluntary or public sectors, who support the principles and practice of community development.

Yorkshire and Humber Regional Forum
Suite D10, Joseph's Well
Hanover Walk
Leeds LS3 1AB
Tel: 0113 394 2300
E-mail: office@regionalforum.org.uk
Internet: www.regionalforum.org.uk

One role of the Regional Forum is to help regeneration projects, partnerships and schemes to build community participation into their work. It uses the Active Partners' framework of 12 benchmarks for communities and public policymakers to assess the extent to which community participation is taking place.

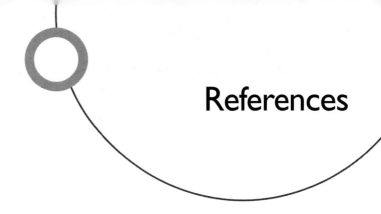

References

Bell, J. (1992) *Community Development Teamwork: measuring the impact,* London: Community Development Foundation (out of print)

Chanan, G. (1992) *Out of the Shadows,* Dublin: European Foundation for the Improvement of Living and Working Conditions

Chanan, G (2003) *Searching for Solid foundations: community involvement and urban policy,* London: Office for the Deputy Prime Minister

CRU (2004) *Firm Foundations: the government's framework for community capacity building.* London: Civil Renewal Unit and the Home Office

Gilchrist, A. (1998) 'Connectors and Catalysts', *SCCD News,* no. 18, pp. 18–20. www.cdx.org.uk/resources

Gilchrist, A. (2001) 'Strength Through Diversity: a networking approach to community development', unpublished Ph.D. thesis, University of Bristol.

Gilchrist, A. (2004a) *Community Cohesion and Community Development: bridges or barricades?* London: Community Development Foundation

Gilchrist, A. (2004b) *The Well-Connected Community: a networking approach to community development.* Bristol: The Policy Press

Henderson, Paul (ed.) (1995) *Children and Communities* London: Pluto Press/Community Development Foundation/Bradford and Ilkley Community College

SCCD (2001) *Strategic Framework for Community Development* Sheffield: Community Development Exchange

Taylor, M. and West, A. (2000) *Signposts to Community Development (Second edition),* London: Community Development Foundation

Further reading

Banks, Sarah, Butcher, Hugh L., Henderson, Paul and Robertson, Jim (2003) *Managing Community Practice: principles, policies and programmes,* Bristol: Policy Press

Crow, G. and Allan, G. (1994) *Community Life,* Hemel Hempstead: Harvester Wheatsheaf

Field, J. (2003) *Social Capital,* London: Routledge

Halpern, D. (2005) *Social Capital,* Cambridge: Cambridge University Press

McCarthy, H., et al. (eds) (2004) *Network Logic: who governs in an inter-connected world?* London: Demos

Mayo, M. (2005) *Global Citizens: social movements and the challenge of globalisation,* London: Zed Books

Nohria, N. and Eccles, R.G. (1992) *Networks and Organisations: structure, form and action,* Boston, Mass.: Harvard Business School Press

Skinner, Steve (1997) *Building Community Strengths: a resource book on capacity building,* London: Community Development Foundation

Skinner, Steve (2006) *Strengthening Communities: a guide to capacity building for communities and the public sector,* London: Community Development Foundation

Skinner, Steve and Wilson, Mandy (2002) *Assessing Community Strengths: a practical handbook for planning capacity building initiatives,* London: CDF

Taylor, M. (2003) *Public Policy in the Community,* Basingstoke: Palgrave

Taylor, Marilyn and West, Alison (2001) *Signposts to Community Development (Revised edition)* London: Community Development Foundation

Trevillion, S. (1999) *Networking and Community Partnership* Aldershot: Ashgate

Willmott, P. (1987) *Friendship Networks and Social Support* London: Policy Studies Institute

The 2nd Secret
DIARY OF
JOHN MAJOR

Published in Great Britain
by Private Eye Productions Ltd
6 Carlisle Street, London W1V 5RG
in association with Corgi Books

© 1993 Pressdram Ltd
ISBN 0 552 14177 1

Designed by Bridget Tisdall
Printed in England by
Ebenezer Baylis & Son Ltd, Worcester

Corgi Books are published by Transworld Publishers Ltd
61–63 Uxbridge Road, Ealing, London W5 5SA
in Australia by Transworld Publishers (Australia) Pty, Ltd
15–23 Helles Avenue, Moorebank, NSW 2170
and in New Zealand by Transworld Publishers (N.Z.) Ltd
3 William Pickering Drive, Albany, Auckland